Writing Spelled Out

By Anna Shenton

New addition 2017

You can discover more about Anna at
http://www.amazon.co.uk/Anna-Shenton/e/B009MO4JHU

Introduction

Writing Spelled Out is designed to show the beginner how and where to start writing. Explained in simple terms with exercises and samples this book will guide you through each step in turn, on what to write, and how to discover who to write for using special techniques

****

Contents

Contents continued

****

Chapter one

Start With A Letter

Fancy getting your words into print but not sure if you're up to it, or where to start? Answer - *the beginning*. It really is as easy as a b c.

Stand back and take a look at yourself. What are your interests, hobbies, and lifestyle? What do you like to read? There you've started. Not that difficult! All you have to do is write a brief description that summarizes the characteristics of yourself. A biography if you like. Make a list, analyse yourself. You may think that sounds silly. You know everything about yourself, of course, but getting it down into a document will help refresh your mind, throw out all kinds of stuff that's been lying dormant in the grey matter.

To produce interesting reading we have to be an interesting person. Often good material goes unnoticed that's all around us. You'll be amazed at what battles its way through onto your keyboard and how it will play a big part in your material. Everyone has something to share with the reader self-analysis brings results. You the author are the most important thing to produce an exciting and interesting read. Your life and experiences, your family, are a sound place to begin. No other, will match what you write because it's part of you alone.

Here is a sample of a self-analysis.

Lucy Smith aged twenty seven.

Had a rough start in life. Parents split and I spent the first fifteen years going backwards and forwards between homes. Having got that out the way I can emphasise the fact that my determination to survive and come out un-bruised was strong. History was not going to repeat itself! Happy now with a wonderful husband and an adorable three year old daughter I love life.

Family life - *yes loads of experience - relationships, emotion, good times and bad.*

Education, Career, - *basic schooling, one year at technical college, beauty and nail therapist, back to evening college, NVQ 4 nursery nurse.*

Personal interests - *shopping, healthy cooking, dining out, homemaker.*

Hobbies - *swimming, knitting, dancing and keeping fit.*

Goals- *have another baby, make lots of designer knitwear, a bigger house with massive garden, and reach my golden wedding anniversary.*

Taking into consideration everything on Lucy's list she has plenty of scope for putting together Fillers, Letters and Articles for numerous magazines, or any other form of publication, mentioned later.

Sticking with the main aspect of writing for the moment we can now cover what to write about.

Branches can be formed from many of the things listed above - pluck out *shopping* for instance - this could cover a multitude of opportunities - food, fashion, babywear and furniture, all popular subjects for Women's Commercial Magazines and more. Browse round a newsagent's stand; see how many publications you could possibly contribute to. In particular, look at hobby, trade and specialist magazines.

You should be able to write anything including saleable articles for a whole range of publications. Bear in mind you don't have to be an expert, because you're not writing for other experts, just ordinary people.

To keep things simple we will firstly look at writing for the letters page, but not just any old letter! So what is the key formula to writing a Star Letter?

Don't be put off by the word *letter* as mastering the art of letter writing brings many lessons for all creative writing demands. Possibilities of achieving publication are high; it can also be quite a lucrative side-line considering that few words are used. If I'm honest it is one of my favourite pastimes and it shows in results. Shortly I'll be bathing in an Elizabeth Arden bathtub relaxing with my free subscription magazine soaking in the aromas or Green Tea Oil.

The demand for readers' letter pages in newspapers and magazines is great and wide-ranging.

The amount of cash publications pay varies, and as you can see the gifts are terrific!

Markets are plentiful and often contain two pages from contributors. There's room for us all.

It is useful to compile a list for future reference of markets you feel suited to contribute to once you have discovered possibilities. Obviously you will write to magazines you are familiar with, although some knowledge can be plucked out of a magazine to your advantage.

As with all types of material the editor will receive hundreds of letters daily, so how do you ensure yours has the best possible chance of being published? Let's set our sights high, and expect to have four successes out of every six. That's high!

Although planning isn't quite so crucial in letter writing there is still some detective work to be done. I personally aim for women's magazines; I find them to be good markets for family life, which is something we all know. I flash periodically between such as *Good Housekeeping - Prima - Essentials - Top Santé* and so on, taking care not to submit the same piece to several markets at the same time.

Always think big and go for the star letter, nothing else will do. This way you will surely fit in elsewhere at least.

Firstly, read all the letters in your chosen publication, now go back to the star letter and study it in fine detail. Make notes of your finding.

What is the subject? Is there a photograph to support it? How many words does it have?

Is it written in the female or male viewpoint? Is it poignant, or does it contain humour?

Secondly, does it begin with a comment on a previously published article and month of publication? Do all the letters begin in this way?

Examples - *I read your article Safe In The Sun (August issue) - Many thanks for your article I've given up smoking (October)* or do they go straight to the point with - *My son, Mark, recently moved back home - I'm always filled with admiration for people who engage in charity work.*

This is a very valid point; it is imperative to begin your letter to the editor's chosen style.

Thirdly, note the sentences - is the first sentence long or short? If it's punchy and begins with just seven or eight words followed by a longer sentence do exactly the same.

If dialogue has been included then use it. And if ninety-six words make the letter, yours should too, not one word more or less. The editor will conjure up his own caption.

Now we have the basics scan the magazine from cover to cover for everything it's worth. Does anything stand out? Look for something you can relate to.

For instance, I read *Family Circle* articles were numerous in topic but the *Healthy Start* issue immediately caught my eye.

It covered smoking in the home. The results where astonishing and highlighted how children's health could be affected, which is something I'm familiar with. I also noticed that previous star letters had a picture containing the previous month's *Healthy Start* issues.

Note in the sample letter all the things mentioned.

Asthma awareness - *I'm writing in response to the research mentioned in the (Healthy Start, April 2006) which claimed that childhood asthma could be cut by nearly 35 percent if smoking and pets were banned from the home.*

Immediately I have mentioned a previous article. I have also explained briefly what I'm talking about so the reader can recognise the subject even if they missed the original article.

I gave up smoking when I discovered I was going to be a mum. I wanted to give my unborn baby every chance of having a healthy start. But after she was born I started again. I couldn't work out why Sara had so many coughs and suffered frequently with a bad wheezy chest.

Here in the above paragraph, a sacrifice was made, giving up smoking; this makes it interesting to others and incorporates the main point.

I didn't realize my selfish habit was repeatedly poisoning her. Eventually Sara's breathing was so bad she ended up on continues medication.

The letter now portrays a full confession, and this will be in favour because the magazine has highlighted someone to recognise the error of their ways. Exactly what the magazine wants - it backs their research and hands out a lesson to all.

I'll never know if smoking caused her asthma but I'm sure it must have made it worse. My advice to all mothers is to stop smoking and live with a clear conscience.

A piece of sound advice in the final sentence has drawn everything possible out of this piece. The correct amount of words was carefully chosen from a previous draft, cutting where possible.

Previous draft - *To this day I will never know if my smoking had caused Sara's asthma to be so bad, but I think it certainly didn't help it at all. If I had a second chance I would have stopped smoking altogether. I would also encourage other parents to do the same.*

A difference of twelve words in two sentences has made a crisp ending and the correct word count.

Some markets may also favour endings with a word of thanks, and naming the magazine once more.

Such as - *Thank you, Family Circle, for helping me see the error of my ways.* If so, be sure to follow suit.

You will be presenting a layout of the editor's choice, not copying; it will be totally your story, your words and should slot in like a jigsaw puzzle. Naturally we can't all have this type of story to tell but if you look hard enough and brainstorm your knowledge you will be sure to come up with a genuine letter in your own right. A letter I wrote similar to this one made star. But even if your letter is just one of several on a page don't be too disheartened, it is still an achievement.

I have found that approaching markets with a single letter at one given time to be more successful, as opposed to submitting several letters at once. Most markets except e-mail submissions making it more efficient.

If you want to beat the deadline when you've spotted a perfect topic for a certain month speed is the essence. Get it done! If *Homemaker* comes out on Wednesdays get it Wednesdays. If you choose to have a few subscriptions, naturally, it will hit your doormat sooner but be careful not to submit - as I said before - too often.

Payment after publication will vary. There is no set time but it is usual to wait three months for a monthly publication or four to six weeks for a weekly. Be patient as I was and numerous checks and gifts will start to roll in.

A surprize knock at the door brought me £55 worth of *Organic Surge Skincare Products* from a star letter I wrote to *Natural health.*

A simple letter praising the magazine for pointing out in a previous article, that exercise wasn't just for the body, but also for the mind.

As you become more familiar with letter writing it would be useful to devise a chart incorporating markets, dates and success rates as this will help to keep exact publications and ensure you don't submit to the same market too frequently. Set yourself a goal of three or four letters a week and it won't be too long before your words are published. Your spirits will be lifted and you will be raring to go with your next piece of work.

Browsing your newsagents or checking the list of *Letters To The Editor* in the *Writers' & Artists' Yearbook* will provide a good starting point. Keeping an up-to-date edition is imperative as things are changing all the time.

So there you have it, no excuses, start writing your letter. Have a go!

*****

Fillers (short pieces 200 to 400 words). Fillers are used to fill spaces at the end of a page for magazines and newspapers and can be as equally lucrative and fun to experiment with. Follow the same principle as for letters. Some magazines have special pages where these items are gathered together.

Get flicking through those magazines and read! read! read! to discover what everyone is talking about.

Be sure to aim specifically at a targeted market. Even fillers vary their requirements.

Opportunities are endless for other short pieces. Magazines often run New Series, and Special Topics, weight issues and diets are always floating around. You might have a success story of your own or a friend maybe. In my case I scooped in £100 from Chat when I revealed how I lost a couple of stone, great! Magazines often ask for *Your Story* and offer great amounts of cash in return. *Send us your pictures* are another page used regular. *Funny things your pets or grandchildren do.* Some markets ask for *Top Tips*, around the house or for cleaning.

Here is an example - Send Your Hair Queries to Take A Break

When my granddaughters visit, they love to play with my hair. Each in turn they pull and tug at the comb and fill my head with endless bobbles. As my hair is permed regular I'm concerned if such treatment could lessen the life of the curls. I'd be grateful for any advice on making my perms last longer.

These types of filler sometimes only need few words but carefully crafted can make good little earners and bring in some great prizes. This short piece –fifty eight words – made a handsome £30.

Ok, it's not all about cash but it certainly helps any writer fighting to make their way in.

When you get lucky and see your filler/query in print don't be surprised to see a slight change in your words. The editor has the right to edit your piece. It's a great way to broaden your market study. The more you write the easier it gets.

*****

Chapter two

Know Your Markets

Letters and fillers safely tucked under our belts and confidence enriched we can now go a little deeper. Like letter writing any form of writing takes the same route. Now we need to analyse potential markets in far greater depth than letters and fillers if we are to write an outstanding article. But don't worry it's not as difficult as it sounds!

Presuming you have now found a publication you feel happy to contribute to, naturally, you need to establish whether or not they take freelance material. Read several consecutive copies of a magazine, you will usually see which names appear regularly at the bottom of articles. If for example, a gardening article is written by the same person every week, you can be fairly sure that this author is on the staff of a publication. Another way is to consult your *Writers' & Artists' Yearbook* which provides a handy guide as to whether a publication accepts work from freelance writers, and also offers useful guidelines.

Writers' guidelines are an essential part of success. But we can go one step further.

Although the basic criteria is paramount there is much more to be discovered by analysing a market in greater depth. Compiling your own file makes it unique. Every detail you've spotted is first-hand and adaptable to the editor's needs.

Personally I'm much happier to submit work knowing I've built an overall picture of requirements. Advice - study a market before submitting any manuscripts, just as we paced ourselves through the letter writing. It makes sense and brings results. Skimping through one issue half-heartedly is most certainly not going to help you produce an outstanding piece that looks ideally suited to slot into the editor's next issue.

So how do we make our work stand a better chance of success? *Answer* - Compile a Publications List/file of the markets we feel most suited to (shown in the following short story guide). Again, taking into consideration our own life experiences combined with occupational knowledge and interests.

Each market has its own special needs. It is imperative to gather as much information as possible and deal with one market at a time to avoid confusion. Studying every letter, filler, article, poem, short story, listing every detail is sure to push you towards the top-end of the ladder. This will give you a good insight to what age group you are writing for and their preferences.

Most of all you will discover exactly how the editor pleases his readers.

Editors are always on the lookout for new talent that can produce good refreshing articles and stories.

By fulfilling detailed requirements, achieving publication will be more likely and worth your efforts.

Before attempting to write a short story take a look at the potential in writing articles. Refer to your self-analysis list and consider using one of your hobbies or interests as a starting point. Writing about what you know will be a huge bonus. You already like the subject and have inside information from your own knowledge on the subject. But do keep an eye on your chosen market to make sure there hasn't been a similar topic recently. It could lose your possibility of getting published if your timing is wrong. Lucy for example is into keep fit. So there's your theme in mind now collect a few extra facts from other articles, newspaper cuttings etc. for ideas.

Keep a notebook at hand and jot down anything that you think will enhance your article and offer a different slant to any particular subject.

Visit your local health club, gym, running group, or fitness class etc. and have a chat to staff and members about *everything* you set your eyes on.

Having something fresh to say makes your article more saleable.

Maybe they are trying out a new exercise program; dance even, such as the Zumba! They could be having a visit from a special guest, if so ask if you could attend and write about it. Take photographs! If someone has received lottery funding for a special event that's even better, be the first to know.

success with receiving lottery funding for a group set my keyboard alight and made ral publications. Keep in touch with what's going n. When using facts make sure they are accurate, the editor will discard it immediately if he spots something incorrect. Remember he has thousands to choose from.

Having all the material in hand you are ready to scour the shelves for that specialised market - in this particular field - if you haven't already done so. Similar to the letters page, the big hunt, should find your market relatively easy.

All set to go, you are ready to analyse the editor's style. So what are we looking for?

A catchy title. Is it a statement? Is it a phrase or just one word? Did it make you laugh or is it startling? How many words are used?

Does the first paragraph have a special way to grab the reader?

How many words do the articles contain?

Count the paragraphs - are they all similar in word length?

Check out sentence lengths.

Is dialogue used?

Are articles factual or theoretical?

Is a statement portrayed in the last paragraph?

Do photographs or diagrams support the article?

Is there a tips or fact box?

Are reference books named?

Happy with your research you can now put an attractive article together. Write with authority. Be clear and precise, sticking closely to fact. A potentially good article can sometimes be spoiled when the writers' emotion or own opinion leaks in too much. Get straight in with a punchy paragraph, which will entice the reader to continue reading.

Don't expect to come up with a perfect master piece after the first draft. Get everything written down, and then play with it. Your voice is there with all the facts and what you want to say, now look closely at the order of your words, sentences and paragraphs. Shuffle – cut and paste – make sure your information is coming out in the right order. Be sure of a *grab you* beginning - sometimes a question. Hopefully there's a point in your article which is intriguing which could be ideal to make the beginning irresistible. You are attracting the editor *before* the reader here. Now move on to the middle or body if you prefer.

You've just made a dramatic entrance with that snappy beginning. The first paragraph is full of promise which must be fulfilled.

This is where you off-load that all important message. Think logically from one aspect to the other and your article should unfold naturally. Remember don't leave anything important out.

A good positive ending must tie-up all loose ends. It could go back to a question posed in the beginning or it could be speculative – looking to the future. A weak ending can spoil a good article if you just recap on the main text. And if dialogue is present keep it sparse. You may have used dialogue to present your beginning effectively. Although it does breathe life into a piece it can also overpower.

Now chop and cut a second time reducing your word count as I demonstrated in letter writing. Proofreading goes without saying; no one wants to read misspelt text and bad grammar, if you feel happier, get someone to scan your work. Finally are you satisfied with the overall presentation? Try to show consistency in paragraph lengths and use the correct line spacing requested – often double for hardcopy and singe for soft. It's a piece of creativity. Make it look like one.

Feeling pleased with yourself; you're ready to double check how each individual market accepts their submissions, the norm usually favourable via e-mail.

Often you will see a comment at the end of the magazine's *Publisher, Print and Distributor* details stating *For Submissions visit – followed by the appropriate website.*

A query letter can sometimes be requested. It can be beneficial if you want to sustain success in article-writing. A polite letter stating your ideas and asking for preferred word count shows your competence.

Don't ramble, keep it sweet, mention any illustrations you have to accompany the article, and any specialist experience you have in that particular field, you may snap-up a commission. Other markets don't insist on queries; merely ask for submissions to be accompanied by a covering letter. Any brief detail of your writing background will always enhance chances.

Your best source for submissions criteria is directly from your magazine. You can also consult your *Writers' & Artists' Year book* or similar reference books. If you are planning to write material for online follow the same steps.

Once you have submitted a piece don't hang around waiting and wondering about the outcome. It could be a few months before you hear anything. Move straight on with your next idea. Time is the essence.

Don't be scared if your article is *rejection*, it could be for many different reasons. Maybe another writer had just piped you to the post, or the subject had already been covered a few weeks prior.

 Deal with it, take it on the chin, learn from it and keep writing. It's what you love to do.

On a brighter note, when you receive the news from the editor that he/she wants to use your article in the next edition all your hard work will seem worthy. But do discuss with the editor Rights. State, in writing, that you are selling only First or Second Serial Rights *not copyright*.

For instance – if a magazine has paid for your article you will still be able to sell to a newspaper so long as you haven't assigned copyright to the magazine. Copyright is a complex issue. Consult your reference book to seek further advice before any commitment.

Celebrations came in the form of a leap-for-joy and a bottle of wine when my first article was published in Modellers' World. It is known for females' to fly model-aircraft but to fly and write about it was in my favour, it was unique.

With that in mind and a perfect title *A Birds Eye View* the editor just couldn't resist reading my article and publishing it with great warmth.

Confidence in abundance, moving swiftly on, I spotted a *What's Your Story* in *Practical Caravan*. A 1,300 word article, on a great caravan holiday set my sails blowing.

 All the material was in my head together with some brochures I'd kept, restaurant receipts and great photos I'd taken.

So what are you waiting for! And once your foot is in the door send another article to the same market, they will remember you.

In the short story market you need to read at least twenty-five to thirty stories before setting out your file.

Firstly, how many words? Our guidelines are likely to read 1,500-3,000 words.

That's ok but we would like to be a little more precise, so get counting and list how many stories you find to have 1,500 words, how many 2,000 words and 3,000 words. Once word favour is clear move on to which viewpoint the stories have been written in. Do they favour first person, or the third person?

Out of thirty stories you read, nineteen may have been written in the third person, and eleven in first person; this indicates that the editor takes both but slightly favours third person view point.

It may seem like a painstaking process but as we move on, the picture in your file will be much more informative than guidelines alone and well worth the effort. Now you can study the plot, concentrating on the overall emotional effect portrayed to the reader. It could be anger, happiness, resentment, romance etc. You may find that most stories favour romance. Once you have discovered the emotion you will establish the theme. Each story relates to something in life. You will recognise that emotion and theme work closely together.

The top of your file will ideally look similar to the next sample.

Market: Take-A-Break – thirty analysed

Word Count: twenty three – 1,300, four – 1,800, three – 2,000.

Viewpoint: nineteen – third viewpoint, eleven – first viewpoint.

Emotion: five – amusement - happiness, four – fear - horror, six – pity, fifteen – pleasure – recognition of familiar experiences or seeing the baddy suffer.

Theme: two – sentimental, eight – humorous, seven - self-sacrifice, eight – love in partners, five – love family, etc.

Making the editor happy means learning how to pick out important points that are common in all stories.

Characters always come first! How many main characters are used in each story? How many background characters? What age group are they averaging and do they favour female or male? What do they do for a living? Are bank managers involved or doctors? Are their names ordinary? Do they travel in the story? Or are most scenes set in one particular area or room? Maybe they live in city or the countryside. Are the characters mainly married, single, widowed or divorced? Do children appear in the stories or are animals involved? The list could be endless.

The more stories you read, the common factors of individual markets will become easily noticeable and you will begin to know them inside out.

You could continue your file as follows.

Main characters Used: seventeen – two main characters, one background, **thirteen** – one main character, three background.

Main character's age: fifteen – 25 to 35, **twelve** – 35 to 45, **three** – 55 to 75.

Occupations: six – secretaries, **ten** – housewives, **three** – nurses, **four** – teachers, **seven** – shop assistants.

Once you have discovered the most favourable type of characters you can then discover if the editor likes publishing stories with love scenes or maybe dramatic action etc. And how does he prefer his stories to begin? Do they tend to begin with action – dialogue? Or maybe scene settings? How much dialogue is used throughout the story? Is it language you relate to easily or are you flicking through the dictionary every five minutes? Are seasons often included?

Establishing the popular beginnings leads to the most important endings. This is one of the most explanatory things listed in the guidelines so you shouldn't have too much trouble; even so, there is always room to add that personalised information you have spotted.

Is there a moral in the final sentence? Does it come to an abrupt halt? Is the twist a good one? Does it leave you thinking you would like the story to continue? Are you totally satisfied with the outcome?

Markets change their tack and style to suit readers' trends. Therefore, reading a couple of issues every three months and adjusting accordingly saves time later.

Although it may seem that stories could turn out stereotype, I can assure you they are all different.

We add our own flavour, conflicts, dilemmas and outcome to make our manuscript totally individual.

You could round off your file for efficiency, to suit the following sample for any typical market.

Words: 2,000

Viewpoint: third person

Emotion: pleasure

Main characters: two, age group: 35 to 50 male and female.

Professions: housewives, average working-class males

Marital Status: single

Background Characters: five mixed age group

Children: favourable

Scene Setting: work place

Beginnings: action dialogue

Endings: happy, refreshing, no loose ends

Well there are your results. Compiled by yourself, through your own personal findings, you will not find a more comprehensive file than this one.

****

Chapter three

Daydream A Story

Magazines well analysed, you should have a good starting point for your own story.

Bearing in mind the ages of your characters and the traditional bias of stories, you should begin to think about how you will write your stories. Keep things simple and unpretentious in structure and choice of words. More impact is created by using direct words. Complicated grammatical structures and long words get in the way of the reader grasping the sense of what you are trying to say. But before we learn the art of structure we need to conjure up a story.

We start with an idea, get the basics down rapidly then revert back to the beginning to see if some sort of sense is recognisable from our flurry of madness. The first couple of sentences chopped and shuffled around a few times suddenly emerge into something likable and begin the paragraph portraying to the reader what we want to say, setting the scene appropriately. So how did we do that? *Answer* – by activating the mind and imagination of course.

Initial ideas for most of us come relatively easily but to make a manuscript interesting, factual, exciting, believable or creative we need to *think things through.* Think things over and jot them down.

Even if your thoughts are mundane to begin with, imagination will soon spark a light, then set your thoughts into motion and drift into a daydream.

I've been nicknamed 'daydreamer' by my husband. He says I'm wasting time: just sitting around doing nothing, if only he knew what was going on in my head! I've been caught out in some of the most interesting places and accused of being ignorant, bored, even simple.

Whatever you're doing take your characters, ideas, events with you. Adapting a habit of holding *daydreaming sessions* with yourself will compose a sketchy plan and actuate results.

The mind is a very powerful thing, daydreaming uses a complete range of images, feelings and sounds from your memory. It can conjure up an alternative life and outcome for you characters for instance. Memory is not abstract, it's built from bits and bobs and provides the writer with material, and all we have to do is probe every mortal strand possible. But with that, comes a word of warning, don't allow yourself to slip into living in solitude as a hermit.

It is imperative to keep juices flowing and add to your personal memory bank getting as much on board as possible. So get out there and get involved in as many events, functions, and social affairs as possible with your eyes and ears wide open.

You are probably thinking well how am I going to find the time to do all that in my already busy life?

Don't worry; your daily routine will also throw up a few ideas for good measure. Even half an hour sitting in the park or café can illuminate the exact situations or answers you've been looking for. Listen and watch! Then note! It works for me.

Everyone's creativity is sparked by unique circumstances, so start searching deeply and laboriously into your subconscious with the following examples in mind which will throw out varying shades of sunlight. The power of daydreaming can transform rags to riches. So if you are sitting comfortably, close your eyes: slow your mind down and get ready to lift-off into the unknown.

Using characters for instance – to get the imagination revolving begin with a simple exercise by inventing lives for strangers you've seen in the park or café.

You haven't got a clue what this person does, no plots, goals or aims. So who is she? Where is she going? Why is she walking alone? Does she resemble someone you know? Give her a name to shape her image. This will add to or may conflict with your mental picture later.

Bait planted firmly, you can now expand on it. Exercise the imagination, turn your first impressions, thoughts around into different lights, hear what its saying, and play with it. Note down anything interesting, images perceived.

The woman I saw in the park looked pale and fragile, her skin like tissue paper, her grey-hair greasy and thin - like rats tails. She will make a perfect third character in my short story, *Family Inheritance*, once I have taken her up to my domain, and dissected, with what if…? or suppose that…?

A prime example for an exercise is to re-enact in mind an incident that has happened, imagine what the outcome would have been if things had gone differently.

The following example is taken from a short story in progress. The plot is a little sketchy at this point; I need to dress it up, add fire and colour, present my characters vividly and move the story forward. So I'll take Jenna and her mum with me while I sprawl out on the sofa and gaze expressionless at the lounge ceiling.

Jenna and her divorced mum get on well, the dilemma being that Jenna wants to move in with her fourth boyfriend. Mum hit's the roof, it won't work.

What situation can I conjure up to make Jenna see she's making another mistake?

Muddling it around in my head finding several conclusions I try to envisage every possible route by applying *suppose that… or what if..?*

I decide to let Jenna go, but in the meantime because of the upset she has caused, mum rents out Jenna's room to a dear old friend.

On the other hand, mum could have sold up and moved north – or disagreed with Jenna entirely, disowning her – or insisted on moving in with the happy couple to make sure he doesn't do the dirty.

My daydreaming session helped me visualise the most appropriate situation to move the story forward and entice the reader. Jenna and her mum in your head, what does your daydream reveal? Take your time, various scenes will appear and you may find that some elements you originally thought just don't fit. You can then ask yourself; why did her mum do that? Or why is Jenna doing this? You will begin to think further ahead and the story will form into a plot as you guide it. Although, this doesn't mean we should ignore the initial plot, as it is essential to have an early framework.

To refresh your daydreaming delve into your private fantasies, and keep your mind active. Read widely, observe details and study people. Daydreaming also creates ambitions and goals, setting you on the path to achieving these things. It really does wonders for the imagination.

****

Chapter Four

Story In The Making

Armed with your chosen market's file, (editorial requirements) and initial story plot you are ready to structure your story. Characters drive the story. The reader must be intrigued, concerned and like the main character. They want to know everything about this person and how they end up. The reader will be very disappointed if you get something wrong.

It can be confusing if for instance – *Rueben (hero) changes hair-colour halfway through the story or his father was a carpenter and ends up a policeman. Lizzie was twenty seven – but suddenly she's thirty in the space of a week.* Depending on how many characters are in the story it is possible to easily get muddled when you are concentrating on so many things. All your characters will have a background too. Although in short stories, - compared to a complete novel – background and atmosphere are minimal and the characters are one-dimensional with no other personality required other than to move the story briskly to a surprise ending. There is little time in which to develop character in the short story.

Even so, it is good practice to set aside a profile book for your characters before you start writing. This only has to be brief, but once written down, you can refer to it at any time.

Here is an example profile of characters in my e-book, a self-published novel **Seduced By Mind Tricks**

Rueben hero – *twenty eight, single, owns mansion.*

Spiked fair-hair, fair-brows.

Ice-blue eyes, long lashes.

Dimpled chin, square- jaw, high forehead, thick-set neck.

Husky voice.

Muscular - burly. Hands like shovels, meaty fingers.

Likes spicy cologne, and designer clothes, loves oriental food.

Hates – domineering women, warm wine, crowded places.

Favourite colour, red.

Drives black Mercedes.

Mother and father divorced, don't speak to him.

Grandfather, only person he has ever loved.

This is sufficient to keep you on track when writing Rueben's character and traits. Although if you feel happier, write as much about a person as you like, family, goals, emotions etc. It does breathe life into characters and create realism; Rueben in my eyes *is* in the flesh.

Devise a profile for all your characters in the story, remembering to keep it minimal in the short story. Background characters don't require quite so much detail.

Rueben's grandfather, known as pops –*deceased.*

Bushy –wiry grey- hair swept back.

Grey- beard and bushy brows, moustache slightly lighter.

Friendly smiley face with laugh lines and deep jowl.

Same high forehead as Rueben, a flaccid plump fold of flesh under chin.

Yes Grandfather has passed on. But portraits are dotted around the mansion. He is mentioned several times by Rueben. He is real!

Names of characters are intrinsic parts of the story too, and should not seem out of place for their each individual role. Name your characters at the outset, not as an afterthought. Your title should also feel well placed.

At the planning stage you must decide which viewpoint the story will be better portrayed; the first person viewpoint or the third person viewpoint? - *Jonathan's mouth gaped as he opened the door. Or - My mouth gaped as I opened the door.* Do keep in mind your results on your Publications file to the most favourable for the particular market chosen.

Wherever you choose to set your story give it a feel of authenticity.

If you're unfamiliar with a certain place research through guide and travel books, holiday brochures. Even better set your scene somewhere you know. Personal experiences will allow you to add that special small touch, a special smell or sound, the reader will feel you are describing a real place. Using your five senses, sight, sound, smell, touch, and taste can bring a setting alive. A bright sunny day or a mad thunderstorm can be effective to set the mood. The weather is also a great tool.

We want to write a good short story so we must consider *all* of the important elements. Planning a solid structure is another of the main attributes needed. Without structure in the story it will flop. You have already read many stories when creating your publications file and should have grasped the art of structure. The technique used should be well recognised.

The overall aim in any story is to engage the reader's attention and emotions the most effective way possible of course, so let's spell it out.

Swiftly introduce the main character and block out the development of the story with a series of obstacles for the main character to overcome. The more conflict the more intense the story develops, making aims seem almost impossible. Each conflict should be followed by the character's emotional response.

Present each obstacle in a sequence to block out the conflict test.

Firstly – show your character up against some form of opposition followed by what she/he wishes to achieve. Then demonstrate the coming together of characters, the opposition to have won the battle. Show how it effects the opposition and the main character's main aim in the story.

Continue with the main character's response, also in sequence. - Demonstrate the cause, followed with a mental, then physical reaction - tears or facial expression. The final response must be shown with action proving the emotional trait to the conflict test concerned.

Make sure you are satisfied with your conflict and that the reader feels the character has made a definite effort to cope with the obstacle.

The more dramatic and resourceful the effort, the more interest and concern will develop.

At this point you could break from your story planning to practice an exercise, if necessary.

Put two very different characters in a room. Through dialogue, put your characters in conflict with each other, as if showing the reader something of the characters and the main point of conflict, do this by following the structure procedure. Although don't allow it to remove your trail of thoughts form your story. This is also good practice for dialogue. Write dialogue as if you were to *hear* it.

Now follow the opening paragraph from the short story sample, noting the structure.

It was plain to see that mum knew what was in the envelope before she picked it up; it was almost as if she was expecting it.

She rushed into the kitchen looking pale and ghostly then flopped onto a chair. Eventually she reached for a knife from the table and slit open the envelope as if her life depended on it. My mouth gaped; I could see her face already darkened with shame.

"Left a secret lover behind?" Hayley blurted.

I watched with fear as mum's tired blue-eyes filled with tears and spilled onto her cheeks.

"That's enough Hayley," Sonia snapped handing a tissue and patting her shoulder.

"What's wrong?" Reading the letter was too much. Softly crying, mum couldn't speak. Instead she buried her face in her hands.

You will recognise that *the development of the story is blocked*; what is the problem? Firstly the opposition is the mystery letter. The main character's achievement is to cover up its contents. Followed by, the coming together of characters; Hayley's comments, Sonia's insistence. The opposition wins the battle; the letter will have to be read. The opposition is shocked; mum doesn't know how this will affect their relationship.

Main character's response sequence; the cause, she is crying because Sonia is being so kind and she feels she's betrayed her. The physiological effect; she can't speak. The final action she covers her face.

Use these simple types of structure to build up your story. Use a powerful conflict in the final obstacle and demonstrate the main character's emotional trait by showing how she meets the final crisis and what action reveals the outcome.

If your ending is unhappy, her response should be plausible or out of her control. Happy endings allow her to be successful overcoming every obstacle.

Keeping the cause and effect situation in mind will help to master structure.

Read the rest of the short sample, noting as many of the points as possible.

I caught a glimpse of the German postmark. Mum's relatives had cut all contact when she left Germany after the Second World War. A handsome soldier, dark –hair neatly greased and a perfect charmer had swayed her to the point of no return. It had been hush! hush! Ever since.

"Come on mum, please let me read it!" my lips quivering I scanned the paper intently.

My dearest Eleanor, I hope this doesn't bring too much a shock. Ralph, my friend writes English letter for me. Uncle Karl says to me your house in England. I know you have letters for me, but I don't see them.

Many years I am looking for you and now Uncle Karl tells me I can now know my mother .I am five years old when you leave me, and I see your face all times in my head. Please forgive me; I need to know my mother, my father dies three years ago.

I wait for you to telefon 01038-532-375421

Goosebumps pop up on my skin like a rash, "Who is Marko?"

"Do I have to spell it out? He's your half-brother Sonia."

I stared curiously into her eyes, "How… can that be possible?"

"I'm so sorry," she snivelled.

I snatched the letter, "where is he then? I don't believe you could do such a thing," my eyes franticly scanning for an address.

Somehow, finding a second strength, mum jumped to her feet.

"I had no choice, it was different then. I begged his father – my own brother Karl. He was my baby, but I loved your father, I was so young. Don't blame me please…" she broke down.

The middle and ending of the story could turn many corners. If you fancy having a go feel free, keeping in mind the following **essential points.**

Engage the reader's emotions

Block-out story development

Build a series of obstacles

Present your obstacles in sequence

Block-out the conflict test

Show your character in opposition

Immediately show character's response

Make key character's aim impossible

Final obstacle use powerful conflicts

Identify ending use as plausible or successful

Emotion presented vividly in characters is essential. Anxiety can be shown in several ways, breathing being a typical way to demonstrate stress or shock. Facial expressions are another physical reaction, the face can become ghostly pale, drawn, flushed or even hidden completely as the character did in the sample. Tapping fingers on a hard surface is a typical restless movement. Fiddling with something – hair or rubbing of the nose, chewing of the lips. Someone anxious might hold something tightly or appear clumsy spilling and dropping things.

Fear can be portrayed through the thumping of the heart, a fast pulse or trembling of the lips etc. and usually comes on sudden after a shock. When our character was in shock her body flopped onto a chair.

If you're lucky enough to be a character in love you can place them close to the loved one, holding hands, arms wrapped around each other.

Think of your own emotional experiences and draw them into your characters.

One of the most effective ways of moving the story forward is to show a character in action.

Mary swallowed her pills and returned the glass of water to the kitchen where Steven was waiting. She knew if she didn't swallow them all he would put them in her food. "All of them?" a deep frown creased his forehead as he gently prized open her fingers.

"Every one," Mary wiped her mouth and was sure she saw a smile in his eyes.

We have seen several simple actions in these few words. Which have been coloured with a little emotion - *A deep frown and a suggestive smile.*

"Joe, you're not being fair," Miley snapped, slumping into the chair. "I always give in."

Joe carried on flicking through the channels as if nothing more than a decent film was on his mind.

"Joe, are you listening?" she shrieked. "It won't hurt you for once. You don't seem to want to do anything these days."

"I'm trying to watch TV," he jabbed a finger at the screen. "I was hoping for a quiet night in."

Miley glared at him. "I mean it," she stood up and grabbed the remote-control. "If that's the case we'll watch something I like."

A bit more drama here has set the scene too, also using action-dialogue. We don't know much about this couple except for some sort of disagreement, that's ok, we are already concerned about their situation and as the outcome unfolds we will get to know more.

It is possible to tell a good tale in a short story by using well-constructed characters who will act out the story alongside an interesting plot or theme. Although very few words are available to mention scenery, premises, bedrooms etc. enough information was given to set the scene in Miley and Joe's lounge for the benefit of the reader.

So we can see part description *and* the use of the phrase *snapped slumping* which adds *colour* and suggests that Miley is distraught. Adding colour means we are heightening up what is already there in the form of characterisation making it have more effect on the feelings and emotions of the reader.

A very simple way to include subtle characterisation is through your characters words. Using the *Jack said* all through your story will be too dreary and predictable. So, make changes and give an indicator to Jack's character.

"By the time you finish that jacket, the baby will be at university," Jack sneered.

Jack yawned, "By the time you finish that jacket the baby will be at university.

Jack put his feet up on the sofa. "By the time you finish that jacket."

"By the time you..." Jack paused, then blurted out in his deep voice, "finish that jacket, the baby will be at university."

You the author must help the characters in the longer type of story as occasionally, they cannot do all the work themselves. Keep a balance between techniques – the characters can do the bulk of the work providing you set the scenes. Having developed your *believable* characters be sure they are well-orchestrated in their relationship with each other.

 Considering all elements mentioned you can now write your story. *Don't panic if it doesn't come out just as you expected,* **this is your first time**. Follow the same process as with articles, cut, chop and change until you are satisfied paying special attention to the beginning and ending.

It's not set in concrete; you can change things until you know it is good, finishing with that all important proofread. Now you can test the water with friends and family before submitting to your chosen market. Although do ask for an honest opinion, and don't get upset if they offer constructive criticism.

Writers' Circles are always a good way to receive help and support from like-minded people, they know what you're going through. Look online at the Writers' Group Directory for one locally at https://www.writers-online.co.uk/Writers-Groups/ or join an online Writers Group. And there's some fab writers' magazines out there packed full of information.

Writing courses are also an excellent way to learn more and expand further. My personal experience was invaluable. A writing course together with determination has been for me a thoroughly thrilling experience.

Persevere until you're published in whatever form of writing you prefer. Don't be too serious; enjoy every word, letter, filler, article and short story you write. It's great fun creating characters, taking them down any path you choose. You are in control anything can happen.

I hope you have enjoyed reading Writing Spelled Out and it has inspired you to give it a go. I would greatly appreciate your opinion by leaving a review on Amazon!! Where you will also find Writing Spelled Out first kindle addition.
https://www.amazon.co.uk/dp/B00BINZT0E

I wish you all the very best with your writing!

Meanwhile please enjoy a complementary synopsis and first chapter of my New Addition debut Romance Novel Seduced by Mind Tricks.

Synopsis

Lizzie Brand - a glamorous self-assured hot stone therapist - is sailing back to England after living the past eleven years in Germany. Lizzie wants nothing more than to start her new job at a London Spa Resort, and trace her long lost brother but finds herself in unforeseen circumstances, only to be allured by the hero.

Already running away from one diamond ring, will she have to resist another?

Reuben Portland - a husky yet sensual alpha male, is out to fill his rundown mansion, with glamorous staff. Reuben a compelling-charmer goes to all lengths to get what he wants.
And Lizzie Brand is within his grasp on-board Ship Davina, on return from a business trip.

Emotions electric, blowing fuses, sparking fires and setting alight red-hot passion that surprises everyone!!!
Although this book resembles a Mills and Boon type romance, it is completely heart warming, passionate, individual, and full of body with real life like characters.

This book is close to my heart, although fiction, it also contains some real life experiences of my own!

I dedicate this book to my wonderful mother, Martha Elizabeth Helen Richards, born in Hamburg, who then, spent the rest of her life
loving and caring for her children in England.

****

Seduced By Mind Tricks

by

Anna Shenton

Chapter One

Lizzie Brand climbed the stairway to deck eight
following the arrows towards cabin 6106 on The Ship
Davina. She dropped her overnight-bag on one of the
bunks and made her way back on deck.
 Gripping the handrail as the engines hummed, she
watched the swells intensify in the glistening North
Sea, and the autumn evening sun weaken.
Had England changed over the past eleven years? She
wondered.
 Part of her ached, but at the same time, her heart
raced with excitement as she watched Esbjerg Port
reduce in size until out of site.
 She had been happy living in Hamburg with her
Grandma, Uma, but when Marco, turned up with a
sparkling diamond engagement ring she knew it was
time to leave. Living in the apartment above, Marco,
had watched her grow, from a shy gangly teenager
into a beautifully curved twenty-four year old, with
long dark hair and legs that went on forever. And he
wanted her.

She'd told him more than once she wasn't sure, there was so much she had to do and hopefully remember. At last… she inhaled a deep breath of sea-air.

"Hiya," a husky voice crashed into her thoughts. "I don't wish to intrude; you obviously didn't hear the announcements for dinner!"

She turned swiftly and glared at what looked like an immense masculine form, against the now slightly darkened-blue sky.

"The announcements were in three languages," a frown creased his forehead. "Hope you understood one of them? Sorry, I'm Rueben," he stepped closer and thrust a hand forward. "Rueben Portland."

There was a moment of silence, before he went on, "Danish… English… German, perhaps…?"

"English, and German, thanks," Lizzie retorted in defence with a sharp German accent, ignoring the handshake, looking hard at his face and noticing how attractive he looked.

How dare this complete stranger surmise that her language skills were so limited?

"I was just about to look for the restaurant," she tamed her thick dark ponytail from the wind and held onto it, "not that it's any concern of yours."

She strode across the deck and pushed at the heavyweight door. Rueben on her heels took the strain with ease. She couldn't help noticing his tanned biceps, bulging from his rolled-up shirtsleeves as the door wafted a spicy–fresh aroma to her nostrils, which he'd clearly overdone.

"Allow me," a smile spread across his face, "don't like to see a lady struggle.

51

You'll find the restaurant on deck seven," he gestured for Lizzie to walk ahead down the corridor. Now in better light, she could see where her initial thoughts on his good- looks had emerged. His ice-blue eyes, crowded with lashes, soft against his lightly- tanned face and cropped fair hair, sent an annoying wavering sensation through her body.

So what! Who is this guy anyway? She thought feeling flushed. The last thing she wanted right now was some hot muscular male harassing her.

The most important thing was to arrive at Elle's house in London, who'd been so kind on the phone explaining living arrangements and giving her the run-down on The Sensory Spa. Clients were already lined up for her hot stone therapist skills.

Everything she'd worked for and planned, over the past couple of years, was now a reality. And if she was lucky, she might get a glimpse of her younger brother, Jake, who she hadn't seen since she was sent by her farther, to Hamburg.

Heading towards her cabin, Lizzie dug into her handbag for the key-card.

She desperately needed to freshen before dinner, and hopefully shake off Rueben Portland in the process.

Sliding in the key - numerous times - the door still refused to open.

"Allow me," she felt Rueben's breathe tickle the back of her neck, "again," his jovial laugh deafening. "Let's have a look," he took it from her hand.

"Sometimes these things crumple making the job near-on impossible."

Studying it, he pointed to the blue arrow, "You've got it the wrong way," he slid the key in, turned the knob, and the door swung open.

She wanted to say, you again, why don't you mind your own business, but thought better of it. "Thanks, you seem familiar with the way the ship works," her chocolate-brown eyes, being drawn to his lingering gaze.

"It's been a long day, so if you'll excuse me," she closed the door firmly, leaning into it. Her legs felt shaky and her heart flipped into summersaults.

Apart from being annoying, there was something about his presence that stirred her.

Normally, Lizzie wouldn't be so off-hand, but as she was travelling alone she'd told herself to be cautious, and she wasn't in the habit of talking to male strangers.

****

Standing in the shower, she felt the luxurious foamy-lather slither gently down to her feet. Something she'd longed for all day. Heavy traffic had made the drive to Esbjerg longer than expected.

She would have liked to wash her hair, but judging by the churning sound from her stomach it had other ideas. Once settled at Elle's she would get back to her usual glamour routine.

Pulling her indigo-blue-jeans back on and zipping up the same turquoise tunic was as much as she could manage. Smoothing a dab of conditioner over her damp hair, she then tugged through her ponytail. A quick splash of lip-gloss and that's it.

After all, she'd heard that ship restaurants weren't all that special, just a place to eat. She would find a quiet little corner, have something simple, and get an early night ready for her journey tomorrow.

****

A tiny waitress, wearing a black skirt and waistcoat, with a crisp white blouse greeted her as she walked towards the buffet restaurant.

"Good evening madam, have you a reservation?" she unhooked the rope cordon from a well-polished pole.

"Reservation?" Lizzie looked wide eyed stepping down, her foot sinking into a thick-pile dark-blue carpet.

"No, I haven't."

"No problem madam. One person madam?"

"Yes, thank you, that would be great," she answered surveying the scene in front of her. Was there a free table for one? She hadn't realized…

"Follow me," she weaved her way through crowded tables. "Here please Madam," she seated her on the only spare chair at a long white-clothed table. Faces dotted all around; she felt a sinking feeling in the pit of her stomach. Rueben Portland in an open-neck shirt with a thick gold chain glistening around his neck faced her.

"You made it then," he dabbed his lips with a napkin. "Just sampling the pâté." Lifting a bottle of red wine, it splurged hurriedly as he poured into an empty glass.

Glancing at her perfectly shaped oval-face and flawless skin, he added, "It's only house-red but very palatable. Try some?" he raised the glass.

She rolled her eyes in disbelief, all the people onboard and she had to end up opposite him.

Avoiding meeting his cool-blue eyes, she turned her head to the side and saw a red-haired lady that she liked the look of; she would be her get-out if necessary.

"No thanks," she answered icily. "I'll be having fish."

Rueben raised his hand clicking his fingers and spontaneously the waitress rushed over to his side.

"We'll have a bottle of chilled Montana Sauvé Blanc, please," he nodded with a grin, "as soon as possible," he then flashed a note in her hand.

Boiling with rage at his presumptions, Lizzie was ready to explode.

"What do you mean, we? There's no we about it," she snapped, this time looking straight into his eyes without a thought.

"You look even more stunning when you're angry," he told her, his tanned face slightly pink.

"No offence," he jumped in watching her pretty mouth gape further. "Just being polite. Forgive me, I can see you don't travel much, thought I'd steer you in the right direction," he shrugged.

Yes I bet you did, her brain thundered into overdrive. What direction exactly? She didn't have to tolerate his impudence. She would simply move to another table when the waitress returned.

"Ah, the wine." Rueben rubbed his hands together.

55

"Montana, perfect match for fish, in fact I'll probably join you, the king prawns are so fresh they're still wriggling, or shall I have the sea bass?" He lifted the wine bottle from the cooler, popped the already loosened cork with his meaty fingers then poured into two fresh glasses.

"Come on," he beckoned, flickering a gleaming white smile as he held a glass - which looked lost in his shovel-sized hand - in front of Lizzie.

He looked burly, his thickset neck almost as broad as his solid square-jaw, but was he dangerous?

Clutching her handbag on her knee, that stirring feeling – was now burning. She frowned and wanted to say, give me one good reason why I would want to be in the company of a hot-blooded – thirty-something – drooling, male chauvinist. But instead, shakily, she took the glass, sniffed gently before taking a sip.

"Not bad," she licked her lips, then took a longer slow swallow, then added, "Why are you so pompous?" her brown eyes wide and wary.

"Like I said, being helpful," he insisted as if he knew what she was really thinking.

Engrossed with his deep rumbling voice yet furious with herself for allowing such a conversation, her gaze locked with his across the table as if being drawn uncontrollable, which seemed to last an age.

"What did you say your name was?"

"I didn't," she averted her eyes realizing there was something scary going on. "I'm not the talkative type.

"But as it seems we're dining at the same table, it's Lizzie," she told him reluctantly, not giving too much away.

"So Lizzie, now you like the wine, can we eat?

"Food is self-service, there's an array of Danish delights over there," he stood up kicking back his chair.

For a moment her anxiety ebbed. Wafts of hot food brought juices to her mouth, she was feeling ravenous - the last thing she'd eaten was Uma's famous bowl of steaming porridge.

Maybe if she kept to pleasantries during dinner, she could drift-off to her cabin and

Rueben would leave her in peace. What harm would that do?

Besides, according to all the looks he was getting from other women, she was probably dining with the hunkiest man on-board, not that it held any significance.

"Lead the way," she put her glass down.

"I really must literally, eat, then, get some sleep," she said standing up levelling to his height studying his triumphant-looking expression; she didn't want him to think he'd won her over in any way.

"Wow, you are tall... fantastic," he put a slight hand near to the small of her back.

"After you. Starters to the right and mains over there," he quickened his step to her side steering the way towards a stack of large white dining plates.

Although now appearing to be polite, she was beginning to think he couldn't stop himself from saying what ever came into his head.

Evidently he thinks being tall is a compliment when some women might take it as an insult. Whatever, he'd be out-of-her-hair tomorrow.

He picked up a plate. "No starter then."

"No," she walked towards the main courses.

"Mm… what about bagte fiskefilet," he pointed to the brightly-lit fish dishes smacking his lips as if already enjoying the taste,

"Had it on the way over. Beautiful."

Keeping her head down as she observed other dishes she couldn't hold back a smile. He could even speak Danish, was there anything he couldn't say or do?

"Or, what about spegesild med logsovs? - Herrings, in onion-gravy."

"Bagte fiskefilet, for me please, with a sliced cucumber salad," she glanced at the sweaty-faced chef.

"Oh," Rueben's eyes sparkled, "you know what it is then?"

Through gritted teeth, she told him, "Baked fillet of sole sprinkled with shrimps and lemon. Ok," then flashed her long eyelashes hard.

"Right, great, same for me then please," he took the hot plate and curled his lips as if impressed.

They both emptied their plates without another word.

Clattering his cutlery down Rueben Glanced up at Lizzie, "Excellent… Dessert?"

He doesn't stop does he, she thought - taking control - for goodness-sake; who does he think he is? This was a bad decision.

Her head came up and she told him, "I don't eat dessert,"

She pushed her plate to one side.

"As I expected, must be hard work keeping a figure like yours."

Pouring more wine, he cocked his head as if waiting for a reply.

At that moment the waitress cleared the table ready for the next course.

"Let's at least finish this, and have coffee. Anyway, are you going on holiday or…?"

She felt he was trying to guess how she would interpret the question now he seemed to becoming familiar to her responses. She stiffened, how had she let herself encounter a stupid boy meets girl scenario?

Hands clenched and feeling clammy she envisaged Marco's expression - his appealing green eyes and warm tender smile had crumpled painfully when she refused his engagement ring -, and here she was dining with a stranger.

From the day she'd moved into Uma's apartment, she'd looked upon him in a fraternal way – just a few years older than her brother - he'd taken her under his wing after seeing the sadness and confusion in her tiny face.

It had been so daunting, a twelve-year-old having to build a new life in a strange country having just lost her mother, feeling rejected by her father, and torn away from Jake; Marco had been everything she needed.

Then on her sixteenth birthday Marco had kissed her, his mouth sprawled wide across hers, wet and sloppy, his first time she imagined.

Although shocked, it had made her feel warm and tingly. From then on he had taken her out.

She wondered how he had reacted when he discovered she'd left for good.

Had he simply honoured her reasons – knowing she longed to be near her brother again – or had he begged Uma to tell him where she'd gone? Knowing Marco, she imagined the former. Lizzie knew he loved her deeply and would want her to be happy and if that meant he had to lose her he would bare the pain and hope that one day she would return.

****

"Don't look so worried," Rueben's voice softened from its usual huskiness, as if understanding what she was going through.

She lifted her head. "Sorry, I was miles away."

"So I see. Problems? You looked rather serious."

"No nothing like that, just day dreaming," she forced a smile, picked up her glass and took a big swallow. He couldn't possibly be a mind reader too!

"Good, so getting back to our conversation," he rested his chin firmly in his hand.

"Holiday?"

"Oh yes…" she remembered, "No I mean. I'm not going on holiday. I'm moving to London. Start my new job next week," she swallowed another mouthful.

"Sounds exciting. I'll be looking for you in Vogue then will I?"

"No of course not," she felt her cheeks burn.

"What makes you say that?" she said wishing she hadn't the minute the words left her mouth.

Watching his eyes wander over her breasts and resting on her V-neck that showed a hint of cleavage, he said "Pretty obvious don't you think, you've got it all - the looks - the height - and your hair's awesome, must reach your waist when not tied in that band-thing."

Tugging at her tunic and breathing a sigh of relief - knowing she'd left herself wide open – she realised she'd got-off fairly lightly. Uma's repetitive lecture pricked her mind, she must be more careful. But words seemed to flow unconstrained.

"I specialise in sensory and massage. It's gone mad in Hamburg, hot stone therapy, that is, amongst other things and I suspect it's going the same way in the UK"

"Interesting," Rueben's fair-eyebrows almost reached his neatly spiked- hairline.

"You won't know what I'm talking about, but believe me it's become very popular," she added.

"Really," he ran long fingers, across his bristly jaw-line before pouring moor wine.

"Hey," she grabbed her glass with one hand and covered it with the other. "Where did that come from? We were supposed to be finishing it off."

We have, shame to waste the white though. Tell me about this hot… something or other."

"Just a drop for me, then I'm off… to my cabin," she hiccupped loudly, "Oops," she patted her mouth, "I don't normally drink much. I'll have a coffee too; I don't want puffy eyes when I arrive at Elle's."

"German?" she replied as he brought her back with a bump.

"Yes, unbelievable. And how difficult it must have been."

His genuine concern shamed her; he was clearly brimming with compassion, the lustfulness she'd imagined had vanished.

Shocked at her own suspicions, guilt filtered through her body, she saw a kind caring man, and not the hot-blooded male she thought. OK but that doesn't change a thing he had still imposed on her private space and that wasn't on. But remembering how he had looked at her earlier she still didn't want to take any risks.

****

The aroma of fresh coffee wafted to her nostrils. "Lovely, thank you," she wriggled on her seat to allow the waitress room to serve the tray in the centre of the table.

"Shall we take coffee in the lounge it's more comfortable, this seat is beginning to feel like a plank of wood?" Rueben looked sheepish at Lizzie, as if expecting a definite no.

The waitress kept her hands on the tray whilst waiting for a response; fully aware she may throw another mini tantrum.

All eyes fixated on Lizzie she had to think quickly. She wanted to say, you as well, is this conspiracy, to keep me in the company of this man as long as possible, but instead said, "That would be nice thank you."

Following the waitress in single file – who daintily glided along without so much as a rattling cup - they swayed towards the lounge and sat down hurriedly in unison, their backs falling heavily into a curved-back leather two-seater below the window.

"There you are Sir," she put the tray on a small table, "enjoy your coffee Sir, Madam, if you require anything else, help yourself," she gestured to a bar filled with fruit and biscuits and shiny stainless-steel coffeepots, then gave a cheeky smile and tottered away.

Although a little too close for comfort Lizzie still managed to admired the setting, the lounge dimly lit with gold wall lights above blue-leather seating that span round the room, windows laced with royal-blue curtains tied, allowing glimpses of dark rough sea and the sound of a guitar strumming in the background.

Amazed at the elaboration she could hardly believe such elegance on a ship. This must be how it is. Thank goodness she had dabbed on some lip-gloss.

Previously, she had flown to Hamburg – eyes full of tears - with a funny-looking escort that hadn't spoken a word the whole of the flight, nowhere near as romantic as a bustling ship.

The Commodore Deluxe lounge, she noticed written on a doily on the table. "Is this a private lounge?"

As there was no answer she assumed he hadn't heard.

"Milk and sugar?" she took charge, making sure she got plenty of strong black coffee.

"Just milk… What if this Elle doesn't call, what then? And your Gran…?"

The heartfelt sincerity in his voice moved across her like the glow from a blazing fire.

"She will, I'm sure, I'll ring her the minute the ship docks and I can get a signal. I have directions anyway."

"Where to exactly?" he blew on his steaming coffee.

"Oh Middlesex, I have a sat-nav in my little yellow Beetle, it's all programmed in."

She glanced sideways at him, sipping her coffee and feeling apprehensive, will Elle be waiting at the port, will she find Jake, would he want to see her, and now Rueben.

Get a grip, she gave herself a shake, everything will be fine where's that determination that's been battling around inside her for the past two years, her fighting spirit, things will look better tomorrow.

"This is important to me; I must get some sleep it's getting late." She went on, "So thank you for your company, hope your plans go well too," whatever they are, she thought and put the coffee-cup down and took some notes from her purse. "I'm sure this will cover my bill if you wouldn't mind."

"Of course," his face darkened, "But before you shoot, I think I might be able to help."

"I'm fine really, no need."

"I can offer you a place to live," he ran his fingers back and forth over his chain pulling it up to his mouth.

"Pardon," she looked bewildered, "I just told you I have somewhere."

"Yes but it all sounds a bit ominous."

"How could you possibly...?

"Didn't I mention I run a hotel?"

Appearing calm and unruffled she said, "You didn't mention anything."

Although insignificant she was still surprised. "I don't need your help."

"Before you totally dismiss the idea, hear me out, you've got nothing to lose. But maybe a lot to gain."

Though he spoke quietly, his voice held a kind of enthusiasm and excitement, like a child's eagerness to tell a secret, and against her will she found herself obliged to listen.

"Actually it's not so much a hotel," he added casually, "more of a Victorian Mansion, on the outskirts of The Lake District and I'm thinking of expanding the facilities. Ideally, I could do with extra staff."

Uneasy with his sudden openness, and feeling the heat from the closeness of his body, she turned her head to the window and saw, in his reflection, a look that conveyed all the tenderness he seemed to feel for her.

Why would he offer so much to a stranger? Did he have an ulterior motive?

Her brain muddled as she tried to make sense of it. Was he lying? She lifted her chin and turned to meet his eyes with a glare.

"Why would you want to do that?"

"It's simple I need attractive competent staff and it seems you could do with a stroke of good-luck."

Judging by the swiftness of his answer she thought she must have been showing that ambiguous-look.

After a moment's thought, she told him, "It's very kind of you to take me on face value, I appreciate your offer but I don't know a thing about you and I'm quite sure my arrangements are all in place."

His piercing-blue eyes softened and his lips curled into a gentle smile.

"Of course. I can't tempt you then, with your own private suite with sunken spa bath, and a balcony with stunning views over lakes and fells? Or if you prefer traditional, there's the south wing?" He raised a brow.

"If you change your mind?"

She wanted to scream, and say that sounds fantastic, instead, she said,

"I won't."

****

If you would like to continue on Lizzie's rollercoaster journey you will find a kindle addition and paperback addition on Amazon.

https://www.amazon.co.uk/dp/B06VT6FBG8